PRAISE

Immediately, this book in your h.
like all potent narcotics, we are u
next page to keep taking us wher.   ...ed to
go! The hypnosis of poetry radiates   .. with Stephen
Emmerson's brilliant *Big Song*. We fi   ρoet asking what we are
also asking, 'Who follows who on the page. The last of love the leaves
a winding sheet in the trees. We kiss — but our lips are old photos
of dogs.'
    — CAConrad

There's nothing to write about, which is the problem and the
solution. Hence a novel without subject, a form of prayer, lighting
out in pursuit of a vacuum. The writing is sprung at precisely the
right moment in a process of disintegration, unfurling while folding
inward.

    There remains a leap, the necessity of another beginning, reaching
out for a margin whose climate can sanction the act of writing — a
simultaneous inscribing and effacing, an archive of that which simply
cannot be forgotten.

    Big Song is writing silence, never quite arriving, always suspended
at a brink of embodiment. Herein is a perpetually deferred promise,
an eternity of false starts. We are always at the point of crossing a
threshold: glimpses culled from field notes, on toward an unattainable
origin where plot, characters and their causality are renounced.

    Memory here ceaselessly exposes itself to questioning. A sense of
exile and loss is disclosed, vanishing into the bedrock. For my part, I
hear an inevitability, the rhythm of nameless murmur in the breath.
Substance is excommunicated, the event abolished; the essential fact
is that someone was there, mining the peripheral, summoning that
which cannot exist. Whatever share of being was once bestowed is
now corroded (the writer knows this) leaving an empty radiance.
Everything must begin again from scratch.
    — Richard Makin

In *Big Song* there is no centre only the surroundings and the nineteen-eighties and the sunlight and the rain on one side of the street and not the other." This is a book of tracings. Generous with intersections of class and neurodiversity and resonant connections with the natural world. It's a substantial collection of luminous objects and ghostly presences: a dog buried over a century ago near the river Lud, dogs barking on the beach, and on the telly. Much like Lyn Hejinian's *My Life*, *Big Song* explores memory and repetitions, capturing the transience, beauty, and heartbreak of life. 'Big Song is water. Big Song is white noise. Big Song is the last line of a book.' This is a work for both end times and new beginnings.

— Marcus Silcock

Stephen Emerson's *Big Song* speeds by at over one hundred sentences per infinite moment. Clusters of phrases reoccur and anchor the narrative, while gritty industrial details intermix with lyrical nature images and personal memories to blend body and landscape together. Often, we hear echoes of a Beckett-like turnaround, in which news 'begins to melt into our body. We have no body.' This dissolution culminates in the final section of the book, Notes Towards a Resurrection, where the 'best part will go into the fire.' Big Song burns through any notion of conventional Life Writing to present language as the charred shadow of memoir.

— Peter Jaeger

BIG SONG

Stephen Emmerson is a writer and artist. More information can be found here: www.eightox.org and here: @tothemadpoets.

Also by Stephen Emmerson

CONTENTS

ISBN: 978-1-916938-17-5

Cover designed by Aaron Kent

Typeset by Aaron Kent

Broken Sleep Books Ltd
PO BOX 102
Llandysul
SA44 9BG

Big Song

Stephen Emmerson

Broken Sleep Books

BIG SONG

Rain red bricks. Early morning frost. Telephone wires cross power lines under silver edges of cloud. A large dog barks in the distance. White blossom streaming over fields. I did not hear any words. For a long time there were no actual words only phrases and accents without meaning. I changed my mind. Changed my dress. Painted my fingernails under cold stars. Change is best. There are no words. Words are white blossoms streaming over fields. I am writing as fast as I can because I am not sure how long I have left. I am leaving a hurried note at the back of my drawer. Orange sunset in dormer window. A lifetime ago. An image. The disintegration of a photograph. I did not hear any words. For a long time there were no words only white noise interspersed with high frequency registers. Telephone wires cross power lines under a dark blue cloud bank. Carrion crows face the future in the oak tree on the other side of the recently ploughed field. Downpour red blocks. I talk to myself under viral skies. The words are hurried notes carried over huge distances. Time is complicit. The cuckoo in the clock. They can all hear what I am thinking. The disintegration of memory. For the time being clear night sky. For the time being kissing gate. For the time being long white dress. I like to watch because you can see others find their way around the footpaths and the horse fields and the cow fields and then you will never have to find the way yourself. It is of course better to find the way yourself and let others watch you so that they do not have to do it themselves. Towns have more rules and are therefore easier to navigate. You can follow the rain because it falls in different places depending on where you are in relation to the clouds and depending on how you are feeling. A cut crystal suspended from a window latch by nylon string. Prismatic light. Diagonal patterns. Constellations. Time elapsed and for the first time it elapsed. There are pylons in the distance. A line of old oak trees. Sparrows feeding in the recently ploughed field. Big Song is water. Big Song is white noise. Big Song is the last line of a book. I did not say anything for a very long time and I didn't hear anyone else say anything for even longer. Dirty dishes in a dirty sink. We are back there. Here. Back again. Under the dead leaves. Mouse blood on my slipper. The cat kettle the calling back. Here in the nineteen-eighties black bees feed upon the past. There are lines and colours through thick patio glass — the sound of transistor radios — a delicate balance restored. Telephone wires cross power lines under threads of fine white cloud. Car windscreen / heavy rain. The hawthorn props up the broken fence as line autocorrects. Talking about Big Song is like talking to a piece of glass. I am reprogramming the spaces between my fingers. Sunlight picks out dust in an otherwise darkened room. Building conversations one word at a time. Water falling onto water. What happened to last night? The hours exhaled a footprint in the frost — we got so excited about the footprint in the frost — it became the scale of the struggle. Hark hark the dogs do bark beggars are coming to town. The leaves in the trees and the people in the trees and the voices of the people in the trees — and the hawthorn and the blackthorn and the damson and the cherry and the apple. Here we go round the mulberry bush on a cold and frosty morning. We wash our face and we wash our face. We wash our hands and we wash our hands. We wash our bodies and we wash our bodies. We wash our hair and we wash our hair. We scrub our skin until it bleeds on a cold and frosty morning. This is not my body. It is not my bloody body. In class we used to talk about class. I had no concept of class. The teacher spent the whole lesson rolling a stick of chalk between his index finger and his thumb on a cold and frosty morning. Dust in sunlight — winter is approaching. I want to let the horses out and watch them run down the lane but they are not my horses they are lost horses. Poppies deteriorate against the white-knuckle sky. A little dog barks in the distance. The nineteen-eighties are full of rowan berries and damsons — they are full of yew trees and the roots of hemlock. The nineteen-eighties contain no plants because there is no earth and no water in the nineteen-eighties only metal shutters — reversing forklift trucks — plastic bottles and diesel engines. Take off your underwear and stand right there in the middle of the nineteen-eighties with burning cigarette in hand. Hold heads together. Tête-à-tête. Skull to skull. No language.

A dog is barking. It is the same dog that barks in films and TV shows. They recorded one dog for the sound of all the big dogs and another dog for the sound of all the little dogs. This is a big dog. It is the same dog that I heard on television last night. It is barking on the beach. I am looking at the waves and it is barking on the beach. I wish it could be otherwise but it cannot — there is no way it could be other. Memory is a lake. A like a lake. A love. Now fold your thoughts and put them in a drawer. The lake is like. Is light. For the time being hawthorn. For the time being rain. For the time being deer. There are thousands of leaves on the sycamore this evening. They will soon fall into the recently ploughed field. They will not fall because it is spring and there are no leaves only buds. There are flies and bees and wasps and false widows and grass snakes and rabbits and crows making nests in the oak trees and jackdaws making nests in the chimneys. They spray pesticides on one side of the field and not the other and on a warm day you can see a wall of vapour slowly settle against the sun. It is said that hawthorn flowers smell of death. They are unlucky. To take hawthorn flowers into a house is a funeral right. They are edible and so are the leaves. The berries work well as a gelling agent. They keep everything together — they keep everyone together. I am listening to the sound of my breathing. I am listening to the sound of your breath. Clouds of smoke. Sun reflecting off an old dented kettle in a garden. It backs out onto the river Lud. I had forgotten all about the river Lud. I know everything there is to know about the river Lud. There are sometimes trout on one side of the river and not the other and there are bricks and sections of old pipes and bottles and fragments of pottery. The garden is full of smoke. It is full of weed and cigarettes and the remains of a dog buried over a century ago. Nobody in the garden has any idea that there is a dog buried near to where they are standing. Though some of the people are sitting down and they have an idea but they have no idea what it is. They can hear a dog barking. But it is a different dog. It is the same dog that I heard on television last night. I am looking at the river Lud and there is a dog barking. I wish it could be otherwise but it cannot — there is no way it could be other. And then I notice that someone has tied a length of black thread around a branch of willow. I would not have noticed the thread at all but there was something tied to it something blinking in the sun. It was nothing. Only an idea. A hundred-year-old dog under mud and stone.

The branches and the birds and the cars and the rooftops and the factories — they are living in the nineteen-eighties. Nothing exists in the nineteen-eighties. I bite my skin until it bleeds. I bite paper and rock and earth. Big Song points to a distant thing — a light thing — a forever thing along the banks. Along the banks where the mind has no control. Sunlight through copper beech. A speck of dust on old film stock. Lots of lines mainly vertical lines but a few horizontal lines here and there and many circles and triangles upon many other circles and triangles. Nothing is happening all of the time. White white colour of blindness. Visual cortex and drowning. Relief of fungus. Relief of lichen. Relief of sky. A word appears either side of a thought. A thoughtless act either side of a word. There is a body within this book and another book within this body. The pine and the oak and the hornbeam and the cherry and the birch. I am touching the pad of my thumb with my index finger. I am drawing circles. I am drawing circles. I am drawing circles. Lighten the sky. Watch my hand from left to right and lighten the sky. Watch my hand from left to right. There were no dead leaves in the nineteen-eighties. In the nineteen-eighties there were no dead leaves. In the past it was impossible to look back but now with the benefit of hindsight we can see it quite clearly. The planets and stars are melting from the inside out. The planets and stars are melting from the inside out. I didn't mean it the way I said it. But I said it the way I meant it. Circles & circles & circles & circles & circles. When it rains we are water again.

We stand in front of the nineteen-eighties and I tell myself that each particle of sunlight is neither here nor there. My body in the rain dreaming of this. I am wearing a brown and yellow dress. It is how I like to dress. I only ever dress in dresses. I have forgotten where I live. We get into a taxi and drive into a Russian painting. It is not our body — it is not our bloody body. Thread water over fields. Lichen watching clouds gather on fingernails. Concrete posts count horizons. Bramble the sky fragments. Moving first stars in darkness. Blame hawthorn over stubble. Tread things that I do not know. Water voices tree. The low of blue stones. Your tongue was another body. Melted white-matter your breathing becomes flower. Your breath the elder with horses. O crow calling. Control further touch. Under the porch light looking out over the red bricks and the moon and the illuminated clouds and the smoke. Am I to undress in the middle of the bypass with cars streaming past? The dog is looking for language. The dog is language. Woof. Let's bury the bones in the back garden for someone to find in a hundred years. The dog is language. The skin the leaves the branches. Bark rubbings on paper. Dog hair on the carpet. Rain rain on corrugated plastic with birds birds and acorns and dark grey skies where we live and work. Derelict houses and barns and pylons and telephone poles on the marsh. No postcards. No letters. No words. This is different. Muddy little fingers and forgotten dreams.

Baby is breathing heavily.

Baby is crawling up the stairs.

Baby is lifting a knife above its head.

Gradually we teach it to sing and that is how white ball of fat and white circle of fat learn to speak. Baby is eclipsed by the nineteen-eighties and the thunder and lightning and the blue crayon in the kitchen and the mobile phone with cracked screen and the cold coffee and the cold water and the open fridge.

Baby is bathed in orange light.

Grey clouds pass overhead — the edges moving with water. In the middle of a circle you can always draw a square.

Baby says there is no such thing as magic only variations in the intensity of feelings. White ball of fat doesn't like me anymore because I refuse to believe that the stars are in motion and I cannot stop writing the same word over and over again and over and over itself.

The photograph we are looking at: A cloud-bank bordered by an immense white light.

The shark is eating me because I can't let go. If I let go — what? Be eaten? Entire cargoes are pitched into the sea.

We are constructing knowledge from scraps and fragments that we find on the shore — that we find in abandoned houses. If you swallow any of them seek medical attention immediately. Do not induce vomiting unless under the direction of medical personnel. Baby does not like being told what to do because there are waters and winds and rooks and geese and trees and we are the waters and winds and rooks and geese and trees. I am more at ease with rocks than human beings — with cats than mirrors — and with darkness than the nineteen-eighties.

Clematis seeds pass beneath new moon in open blue. I know this one — I know it — I know it not. Look but do not stare. Leaning forwards a body upon the sea. We hold ourselves close to the fire. Mind is body. Slows down. We are wearing pink négligées on stage smoking beneath a fake rain cloud. We look into the drawing the forgotten drawing it is described by an unknown voice. Look but do not stare. Now body over music. We look into the drawing and we forget it is a drawing. It relies on secrecy. Big Song relies on secrecy. Big Song tells us where we should go next and what we should do even if we don't like being told what to do we will do it if Big Song tells us to. Drown in the sea with body in another body. Hold ourselves close to the fire. Mind is body. Slows down. Take turns reading lips. During the summer the flies return. The sparrows. Can you put language in the microwave? There were no books in the house that I grew up in. Or if there were they were unread books. I had lots of good ideas when I was younger but as time went on I realised that most of my good ideas were just bad ideas that I believed in. Right now we are breaking the limits of body. We walk along the beach. We are against the wind collecting driftwood and sea glass and black pebbles and white pebbles and the bones of cuttlefish and clam shells. Where are you? I am right here I am right beside you I am only a few steps behind. It is of no use because they are specific units of structure. The tongue and the lips and the teeth and the throat and the lungs and the air and the image. I stay still I stay absolutely still I am still moving. Rain on his hair. The sparks they rise from the fire. Wet flames. White blossom streaming over fields. Yr words are nothing but dead ash. A face. The faces. Yr words are nothing but ash.

Unwind the thread. Measure the thread. Cut the thread. Morning of still water and crows. Ice and water and crows. Unwind the thread. Clouds gather on the horizon. There is dirt under my fingernails. I cannot count when there is dirt under my fingernails. I have almost no facility for multiplication. Over and over the tides to Dover. The jackdaws are chasing a buzzard away from their nest. The wind through a broken pipe and through plastic bag and through blackthorn and through teasel and through reeds in drainage ditches and through barbed wire. In darkness they blame each other. In daylight they blame themselves. The hawthorn and bracken and reedmace and elder. Magpies low over stubble. The clouds over and over. I turn the spool of thread around in my pocket. It is black thread and I tie it to things that I do not like so that if I forget that I do not like them I will remember that I do not like them.

This is the insects talking. The shiny black beetles and water boatmen they will stand with their lovers and face the system. All blue. As blue as blue. And as water as water is water. The leaves in the trees and the people in the trees and the voices of the people in the trees. News begins to melt into our body. We have no body. This is not my body. This is not my bloody body. The nearest thing that I'd seen to it before was a photo of the back of the eye — when you recognise in the thing that's seen a picture of the receptor that sees it. He likes to make charcoal sketches of trees and then colour them in blue. Clouds gather on the horizon. The other world is ample it changes colour regularly in order to control the emotions of its inhabitants. I unwind a length of thread and cut it. I tie it around the trunk of an ancient willow. They are my favourite trees. Bats feed on caterpillars that feed on willow. Instead of this wilderness we learn to switch off whenever we can. We dance. We dance. Into the morning light we dance. Left and right and left and right over and over and under and under we follow the sun with our steps our steps. We dance. We dance. There is dirt under my fingernails. I cannot count when there is dirt under my fingernails. I have almost no facility for multiplication and therefore I cannot dance. Danger is near O dear O dear. An apology on cold stone. What are skies for? They are for dreaming. They are for beginning and ending. They are for thoughts that the body cannot hold. Danger is near O dear O dear. Over and over and over. Time looked out and melted the details — the words written across the sky in red and white. Change how nothing matters absolutely nothing matters and yet everything matters a great deal. Your breath your breathing — a false earthquake in the distance. The elder about to flower a skylark. Your hand reached out into the best part of this world and suddenly we sang: *If wishes were horses I'd wave them away and if words were branches I'd burn them today. Green grow the rushes O. Green grow the rushes O.* You should never turn back on yourself. It is a sign of being lost. Even when you are lost you should always look like you know where you are going. That way people will be less likely to attack you. My hands are bleeding again. They are bleeding into the river Lud — which is also the nineteen-eighties. The nineteen-eighties are boy and body and water and body and text. I am listening to the birds and the lawnmower and the cars and the electricity substation and the wind in the leaves and the voices of the people in the trees. I would learn to read braille but my sense of touch is in the nineteen-eighties. My hands are bleeding again because I have washed them with wire wool and steel brushes. We scrub our hands and we scrub our hands and we scrub our hands. We scrub. We dance into the morning light. We dance.

Birds. The birds. I pick them up and I put them back down again. Birds are difficult to pick up but they are harder to put down. Have you ever tried to put a bird down? It is more difficult than you might expect. In the same way that climbing down a mountain is harder than climbing up. Writing something down is easy. Anything can be written down. Anything can be written down in the dark. The dark can be written down. It is important to be in the dark when you write anything down. Anyone can be made to say anything by writing anything down. Writing something down is easy. I can be written down. I can be written down in the dark. The dark can be written down. But birds cannot be written down unless you have held them in your hands first because they are sensitive creatures and in this way they are related to stones. When I talk about birds I am usually talking about crows or sparrows but in this case I am talking about seabirds. Gulls. Cormorants. Terns. A coarse red stone mottled with salt and calcium deposits. I throw it into the sea. A white conical shell. I throw it into the sea. A smooth slate-coloured rock with patches of iron oxide. I put it in my pocket until I can decide what I want to do with it. Of course I do not have to decide to do anything with a smooth slate-coloured rock covered in patches of iron oxide. The trees and the wind and the voices in the trees and the leaves and the stones and the sea. A dead dogfish. A dead dogfish upon the stones. A length of blue rope — approximately two metres. There is a language forming — a red language buried within. As it grows sounds are made. Glottals. Dentals. Primal. They are as much a part of the body as the rain is part of the ocean. I put them down and I pick them back up again. Rip up stone. Rip up sunlight. Rip up gorse. I pick them up and I put them back down again.

Begin to extend loss and grey frequency. Are you the same shadow begun to cloud? There are thousands of starlings in the sycamore this morning / front garden. There are thousands of starlings in the sycamore this morning / back garden. Taking turns to feed in the recently ploughed field. Begin with sawdust or knitting needles. Batteries or darning thread. Fear is hypnotic. Time can be controlled by language but it will eventually collapse in on itself. A mirror held under water. Telephone wires sunlight and droplets of rain. It is the nineteen-eighties it is not the nineteen-eighties. Light fell in a different way in the nineteen-eighties. Cold tea. Frost. Breath. Breathe. A single bar of heat. I am going to be quiet for a very long time. Nothing has happened. It is astonishing that no one has noticed. Time is completely empty now. We take turns drinking water from an old coke bottle. To reflect. To pity. To disgust each other. To lose one another's body. There were thousands of leaves on the sycamore this evening. They will soon fall onto the recently ploughed field. Standing water. Marking time. Every conversation is disabled by language. Belief in a plastic dark. Belief in an alternative economy. You remind me of a child. Rain fell in a different way in the nineteen-eighties. Is it still the nineteen-eighties? Telephone wires grey sky and starlings. Let's promise to offer no more names. To name nothing. I am happy to live in the dark. The tides are governed by the moon. We take turns drinking water from a river / from a mirror. It is snowing on the recently ploughed field. I write to leave some black on white. The white glints through the words like waves. One pushing against the other. Snow fell in a different way in the nineteen-eighties. It fell in exactly the same way. I only like the beginnings of things — my shelves are full of unfinished books. Cold tea. Frost. Time can be controlled by language but you will pay for it in non-verbal cues. A line forming. A line buried within. Nothing has happened for a very long time. My dad used to say if you can't find anything important to do find something to do and make it important. The nineteen-eighties were so important. They were no more important than the present moment. The rain is falling on one side of the street and not the other. A puddle forms in the same pothole every time it rains sufficiently to do so. I can remember the feel of the touch of her hand. It was cold even when the sun was blinding. The feel of the touch of his hand was like a dog's paw (the pads) or imagine the hand of a primate. Emotions are transmitted through touch even in the rain. Even if you are standing in a puddle that forms in the same pothole every time it rains sufficiently to do so. Time can be controlled by non-verbal cues but you will pay for it in language. I breathe in starlings all of the starlings flying over the recently ploughed field. Cherry blossom has covered the car. I cannot see through the windscreen. We never go anywhere anymore. Shafts of light. An oncoming storm. A line of pylons in the distance reflect a low winter sun. Thousands of sycamore seeds have germinated everywhere I go I see them growing. Green leaves. A red car. Stars in the sky. The grooves in denim. The wooden arm of a chair. My forehead. I am in this moment counting the things I can see and touch and smell. Breathing was different in the nineteen-eighties. It was almost exactly the same but it was different. Do you want food? Drink? Telly? You must want something? Another person enters the room. It is the same room. It is a totally different room. It is the same. The light changes — there is a granular shift. A moth bursts from the drawn curtains into a cloud of exhaled smoke. The rain is falling on one side of the room and not the other. There is only one side of the room and everything is in it. Later there is nothing in the room but a shaft of light. An oncoming storm. A line forming. A line buried without. Nothing has happened for a very long time and it is happening now. I copy out the ocean with charcoal letters — there are a few footprints in the early-morning frost. There is a large circular mark on the table as if someone has used a scalpel to cut around a shape without sufficient protection. The grain of the wood is reminiscent of an eye under a microscope. An iris. A light-brown iris. The same colour drifting in. A preview of sunset between fingertips. Between fingertips it is still the nineteen-eighties. The nineteen-eighties in the palm of my hand. The palm of my hand rubbing against the arm of a nineteen-eighties' sofa. Synthetic fibres. *This item does not require a schedule 3 interliner. All foams fillings and composites have been tested by our supplier(s) to ensure compliance with the relevant ignitablity test. Covers and fillings are cigarette resistant. Covers are match resistant.* A line has formed on the surface of the table as if someone has drawn a straight line on a piece of paper using a ruler without sufficient protection. It is a deep line that will not easily be removed with sandpaper — or if it is removed — the act of sanding will create a deeper and even less removable mark than the line itself. But I am not going to react to things like that anymore because the trees are still here and the leaves are still here and the sky is still here and the people are still here. Even the good and bad people they are just people and leaves and trees. I can feel my weight through the soles of my feet. They are falling onto the tarmac. They are falling onto the lane with the leaves and the trees and the people. Hawthorn blackthorn wild rose and damson. I am reprogramming the gaps between my fingers. Sunlight picks out dust through a gap in the blind. Building conversations one word at a time. Water falling onto water. The alarms. The floods filled with fool and daughters. What happened to last night — the hours exhaled a footprint in the frost — we got so excited about the footprint in the frost. A cup of tea. A worst lion. The schadenfreude of hide and seek. October follows the ice. It is just the beginning of winter. Our cheeks are red. The words are streets. Coming ready or not. The skin on my fingers is blistered and flaking as if I have been trying to climb out of a deep hole — but I have not been trying to climb out of a deep hole — I have been lying on my bed doing nothing. If you follow this piece of string it will lead you back around to the beginning of this piece of string. To the church bells. To the steeple. To the graveyard. To the drawbridge. To the people. I would spend an unstructured sentence watching you eat in the sun while it rained heavily without stopping for an unaccountable length of time. If you get stuck look at the others it will remind you of what to do. Don't follow the others watch them from a distance and know what to do. I don't know what to do. I'm building one conversation at a time. Our surroundings are unpredictable so we don't burn anything we don't bury anything we only dig holes and gather kindling. In Big Song it is never cold enough to make a fire because we bury ourselves in the ashes of others — of those that came before. Water falling onto water. That is the Big Song. Up the stairs outside your body — backlit in silhouette. Specific details of conversations have faded. I tap my chest five times. Tear the paper in half — tear the paper in half — tear the paper in half — until it cannot be torn any more. The dog and the people and the trees and the red lights of the towers — that is what we are supposed to do with each other — it is an absolute classic — it happens when you get tackled from behind or spend a lot of money. There are loose bits and hard bits and rough bits and smooth bits and even bits that will burn other bits if you are not careful. The absolute dog of the situation is the hair at the back of your throat. I catch thrown balls for the absolute dog — for the council-estate dog — for the dog of Margate and Folkestone and the dog of Lincolnshire. I faked my own death for Big Song in the middle of the nineteen-eighties. I faked my own death. Everybody walked so much faster then because they were not attached to objects — they knew nothing — they had no siblings and everything they did was decided by chance. Not being attached to objects it cannot be proven that they ever existed because people leave traces on the objects they are attached to and if they are not attached to them there can be no trace. People often walk past their memories now because they are not engaged with objects. I freed myself from objects in the nineteen-eighties. I am no longer bound by the conventions of remembrance which means I cannot thank other people enough for my own misfortune. Remember. I remembered that I was born and then I remembered that I remembered being born. Now you see me now you don't. In buzzard and swift and magpie. He painted his face white and then lots of other people painted their faces white because they wanted a face just like his. I didn't want a face like his. I did not want a face at all. I followed a piece of string instead. I followed it for years until I found myself back at the beginning of the piece of string. I am dancing with a piece of string — I am dancing with the leaves and the trees and the starlings. And the people they are dancing — they are dancing themselves free of their surroundings. I am dancing and I am surrounding the surroundings. In Big Song there is no centre only the surroundings and the nineteen-eighties and the sunlight and the rain on one side of the street and not the other. Everything we did was decided by chance and most of the time nothing happened. If you get stuck look at the others. It will remind you of what to do. Don't follow the others — watch them from a distance and know what to do. None of us know what to do. I like being told what to do and then deciding if I want to do it or not. Most of the time I will not do it if I am told to do it even if I really want to do it. This is because Big Song taught me not to follow others but only to listen. Listening is just like doing but without being present. In the nineteen-eighties a dog stands on my tongue.

I spoke to you I speak to you my language. Burnt grass at the edge of a field. It should not feel like moon circling. It should not feel like sun circling. Awake. Rage circling. Again and again and again. Ash falling. It is not my dream. Pollen fading. It is not my dream. It should not feel like sea circling.

Baby says: Dog hairs.

Baby says: Silica.

Baby says: Rich seam of gold running through unidentified rock.

Baby says: All points from a given point traced out by a point. Distance is constant. There is no point that is not equal.

A day together. A bag of laundry. Decay together. A bag of laundry. We light a cigarette but only pretend to smoke. There is a blackbird in the garden defending its nest. Defending it from no one but defending it nonetheless. The laundry smells of smoke and we can barely make out the figures on the other side of the field. We later realise that there are no figures on the other side of the field only square and circle and spirit over. One by one by one by one.

Baby plays trumpet.

Baby learns to swim.

Baby crawls into a box.

Baby is interested in the following items:

Rabbit faeces — daisy — dead nettle — bramble leaf — elastic band.

Look at kettle boiling. Look at rain falling. Look at sea rolling. I put on my dress and baby eats butter. The ocean is covered in tulips. Baby has stolen my flesh. I kiss circles when it does not sleep. I love circles and I learn Italian. *Che ore sono?* I do not know. I have no idea. I am no longer able to answer that question — but who is that knocking against the glass? Is it baby? It is baby. We go on a three-mile run and get sunburnt. My head no longer fits through the hole in my favourite t-shirt. I crack an egg and put my finger in. I will not eat it but I will enjoy trying to remove the blood spot. The broken vessel. What is an egg? Baby says: Ga. Ga is egg. Ga is book. Ga is world and world turning.

Baby says: Apple.

Baby says: Bird.

Baby says: Nothing — I didn't say anything — stop looking at me.

The best quote baby can come up with is: Truth does not require language but language requires truth.

Bad baby. Failure baby. Do better next time baby. Have you grown an extra finger on your right hand baby?

Dust in sunlight. It is not my dream. Mist rising. It is not my dream. It should not feel like sea circling. It should not feel like bird circling. The black dots before my eyes become seagulls. They are turning. Turning turning and speaking in tongues. Biting leg. Biting wing. Eat eat and turning turning. I read a poem backwards and a tree falls down. I'm not sure anything has ever happened before. Did anything happen? Are we happening now? Circles move around each other. Rain and hail and tame white dove.

Baby is a poet.

Baby is a circle of fat moving through space.

I'm sorry baby. I am so so sorry.

Baby is full stop and comma and semicolon.

Baby holds spoon to silver mountain.

Circle of fat writes a shopping list and stares at the sky.

The sideboard is green. There is grass growing out of the drawer.

Circle of fat does not like music.

Why not push yourself into a corner and level up? The table is a discussion in itself. Collect stationery. Three blue biros with red tops. Three red biros with blue tops. Stay still and feel the weight of your own body. Lick the wall. Lick the carpet. Lick the sky with your eyes open and then lick the sky with your eyes closed. This is the firewood we have collected for next year.

Where is baby? Where is white ball of fat?

Baby is sinking through time.

White ball of fat is in kitchen sink.

O circle it is what's outside that counts.

White circle of fat makes a scaffold.

Baby is arguing with the wind.

Today we had Greek yoghurt with honey and walnuts. I do not understand the wind and the rain and the star of Lucifer. White circle of fat rolls the dry latex into a soft brown ball and sticks it to his gum. Baby eats mulberries in the bush with the birds. Look Ma no hands. Baby is excited when the sun comes out. The red square and the blue square are on opposite sides of the room to the black circle. We save up all of the dead flies we find in the conservatory each summer and keep them in a large tin. Descend into flames with white circle of fat still flapping. White circle of fat is obsessed with staplers and Post-it notes and paper clips. I cover the garden. I cover the fire extinguisher. I cover my skin cells. I cover the starlings. I cover the sycamore. I cover the beech. I cover the table. I cover the petrol station. I cover the town of Rye and the headland of Dungeness. I cover suburbia. I cover the covers. I am covered in what I am covering and I am covering what I am covered in. White circle of fat is not impressed.

The sky begins to melt into our body. I am listing the names of the trees and the names of the plants and the names of the people. The sycamore is on fire in the back garden it is turning into ash. The names of the plants and the names of the people are turning into leaves at the end of the day. Smoke and tinfoil and unmade beds. Bare lightbulbs and empty boxes of medication. Xanax and morphine laid in a knife of empty sunlight. Everyone is walking in the same direction. Forever and ever in the same direction. Forever ever. Keep right. Keep moving. Tail between legs in the aftermath. The body begins to melt into the sky. I am listing the names of the bodies and the names of the clouds. A line of poplars almost collapse under the weight of the dark grey horizon. I have a trapped nerve in my neck — there is no pain only the numbing of shoulder and arm and chest. Only numbing. Only numb. He was exactly that but without the blue background. Everything is remembered from the beginning even as it is backwards made. Absorb sunlight. Absorb water. Absorb dust and feathers and glue. It is unmade and made again whilst remaining always intact. What is it? Just? The absence of definition. A word expresses only a path — an animal track — a snicket through the woods. Through houses. Through darkness and light. The particular occurrence of glottal or dental — of speech or disaster of dust. Draw a slow line from here to the end of the page. It is a fine action. A work of extraordinary growth. I lay on my belly aiming the rifle at a distant target. We all did. They told us to shoot and we did so without question. It was the beginning of a war that no one knew how to stop. But I am out of that now — surrendering only to hawthorn and ash and birch. The nineteen-eighties no longer exist. They are yet to exist. There is no sunlight in the nineteen-eighties only a vague sense that something is not quite right. That something is other. Other is the nineteen-eighties. Other is other. It can be no else. In the ocean everything is calm wide open and vulgar. Down to sea and break over hollow tide. Wake to pink skies. Outline of pigeons and telephone cables. Big Song is a landscape of burnt trees and outbuildings in smudged charcoal. Eleven matches in one box and three matches in another. The eleven matches have blue heads and the three matches have red heads. By the end of the week they will all be black. Never let the details get in the way of the facts. Wake to blue skies. Starlings feed in the recently ploughed field. Standing water and fallen trees. There is nothing else. In the nineteen-eighties there are still halfpence pieces. A penny for them. A farthing further along. Door handles only exist in the nineteen-eighties. Corners and ceilings and shafts of winter sun.

Dust the dust floating through space. In the nineteen-eighties nothing has an outline. Bars and lines and static. The upside-down lips of a tree or a Spanish uncle or a fire escape. Escape. Escape. Escape. A line and a line and another very long line. The squares become rectangles due to the weight of the years. The circles are free they are free circles. In the nineteen-eighties there are only circles. I breathe in red light and I breathe out white light. I breathe in yellow light and I breathe out white light. I breathe in blue light and I breathe out white light. I breathe in white light and I breathe out white light. I breathe out white light. I breathe out white light. I breathe out. White. Light. The starlings take turns to feed from the recently ploughed field. The magpies the rooks the jackdaws the crows. They are taking turns to feed from the recently ploughed field. We are magpies and rooks and jackdaws and crows. We are buzzard and kestrel and starling and blackbird. Driving to work I am lorry and car. I am grey cloud approaching from the north-west. I am every single lane on the motorway. What are words for? They are for dreaming. They are for beginning and ending. They are for thoughts that the body cannot hold. The body cannot hold the words for they are also body and body cannot hold another body even if it is the same body. Big Song tells us where we should go next and what we should do. Even if we don't like being told what to do we will do it if Big Song tells us to. We will do anything in order to live in the nineteen-eighties or even to utter a word. I can smell the sofa and the chip fat and the dirty dishes in the sink. We are no longer there. I know that now. The ashes are ice. We are terrorised. An ice author moved by weights and counterweights. There is a star flickering in the distance. A light behind closed eyes. It covers only a single point on the surface but considers itself the entirety of the image. Red car lorry lorry and ice sheet falling. I am crane crane and crow crow and bottle top and coke can. I am dark blanket of cloud. Big Song is rain falling and door closing. It is water and water and nettle. It is moth exploding from curtain. Immediately. All of a sudden. Eventually. Later today. A rook breaks through frozen water in the recently ploughed field. Oftentimes I have reached for the light only to find it is no longer there. No longer there where my hand feels. Where my hand moves feeling for something. For something no longer there. Oftentimes I have stopped thinking only to find I am thought of. Oftentimes I have stopped writing only to find I am written. Stand still — become shadow. We are the equivalent of water. Of circles. Of squares and triangles. Big Song tells me to lie down on my back. To let my arms and legs fall away. To let my torso fall away.

To let my head fall away. Big Song imagines a door in nobody and we walk through hand in hand. We are here at last in the brown beige and magnolia of the nineteen-eighties. One two three on the hob coming ready or not. I found you. Too easy. Stop following me. Crawl further and further away until I cannot see or hear you. Listen:

A line & a line & a line & a line & a line. Then a circle & a star & a circle. Then another line & another line & another line & another line. Then a star & a circle & a star & a circle. Then a space & a space & a space & a space & a circle & a square & a triangle. That look like diamonds. That look like diamonds. That look like diamonds. That look like diamonds followed by a broken line & an unbroken line & then a series of intersecting lines that create a patchwork of squares & diamonds & triangles that eventually become a series of lines that no longer intersect — & then circles & circles & circles.

When you are travelling through time it is all geometry. The twisted symmetry of our bodies reflected on water. The frozen puddles in the recently ploughed field. Circles and intersecting lines being pecked at by rooks and jackdaws and magpies. Points moving in all directions — in tangents that meet in curves and parabolas. Weights and counterweights — an unbalanced line of white light moving away from the silhouette of a human form. The light is heavy. It moves along the structure. A network of pulleys and chains — the masts only realised upon water. The body again. The body in another body. Water. The sea. An ocean back again. Beginning to end no difference. My body in the rain dreaming of this. At the end of the nineteen-eighties they poured concrete over everything. The sycamores and the starlings and the bright morning light. Concrete over everything.

The bright morning light. The body together. Together in one body. Concrete over everything in one body. Body over everything. Over stars and fire. Over train doors and books. Over magazines and ant nests. Over clouds and sofas and antique silver and television sets and radio transmitters and plays and automobiles and sunsets and dancing lights and children and frosted glass and humpback whales and clocks and newspapers and dark matter and paper chains. In the nineteen-eighties they poured concrete over everything and now that we are encased in it we cannot look back we can only lie very still in our body. Together in one body. Body over everything. We are friends with water and buzzards and sycamores. With starlings and sparrows and hawthorn. With foxes and moths and butterflies. Together in one body. Together in one body. We are friends in one body. Our bodies look different in different mirrors. The light.

The angle. The size and shape of the glass. But now that Big Song has become mirror there is nothing left to look at. In Big Song nothing has any weight. For a long time I couldn't say anything at all. I invite you to name it. To say it. Big Song is a brief history of burnt out buildings. Big Song is an unverifiable image from which little can be discerned. Big Song is a square and a rectangle and a circle. I am drawing squares and rectangles and circles. I am dancing and I am surrounding the surroundings. In Big Song there is no centre only the surroundings and the nineteen-eighties and the sunlight and the rain on one side of the street and not the other. I am on one side of the street and not the other. I am dancing with buzzards and rooks and starlings. I am dancing with sun and stars and fire. I am dancing with ash and beech and sycamore. I am dancing with kestrels and rabbits and hares. I am dancing with rain and wind and telephone poles. I am dancing with pylons. I am dancing with water. I am dancing with mirrors. In Big Song there is no such thing as body.

NOTES TOWARDS A RESURRECTION

Owl light over still water. Morning storm. A metallic purple landscape. Shadow of cloud against power station. We hold on to the image too long. Too long against the sea. The red flag of mourning. The stones and pebbles bury each other. Swallow the silence of birds. Why read why bother to read when you can walk it is a form of reading. Crow is a form of reading. Tree is a form of reading. In any other verse I would have moved to insert place name here with insert partners name here and I would continue to exist but in this way I am dust and sunlight and copper beech. This is not the beginning of something it is more like the middle or the end. I know it is not the beginning because at the beginning I wrote about how I prefer biographies to novels because in biographies you always know where you are. In novels there are often too many characters and too many different points of view. In that respect you can read this as a biography because I have not written it myself. Who follows who on the page? Each character a letter written in white space glowing at the margins. Nothing can really follow this. I wake up suddenly in the middle of summer a series of absences stacked up next to each other against a white wall. The stones and pebbles bury each other. A giant dragonfly hovers for a moment and then disappears. I am walking up an external spiral staircase in Amsterdam. At the same time I am walking along Briggate in Leeds. At the same time I am sitting in Kennington Park. At the same time I am watching bluebottles in the conservatory. At the same time I am wiping a spiderweb away from my eyes. Things become what they are thought to be. In real time nothing but shadows. Nothing but a new acquisition. Nothing but a car engine turning over in the dark. Everywhere nowadays no matter how beautiful looks like the kind of place where something terrible is about to happen. And so what if we feel it so? *The best part will go into the fire.* A series of abscesses. Eight burning holes of light in a photograph of the sky. And so what if we feel it so? Outside of myself I am walking in Hamstreet Woods searching the leaf litter for mushrooms. Instead I find an old shell casing from a Spitfire. Instead I find a toy plastic car. Instead I find an old whisky bottle. Instead I find an empty box of cigarettes. Instead I find a Polaroid of a child folded into quarters and I know it is a lost child. I fold myself into the forest until it rains and then I return home. At home I think about choosing someone at random to follow for a whole day. I will write down everything that they do and then I will write down everything that I do in relation to following and writing about them. In my grandad's old Italian phrase book I find a home-made bookmark. A fragment from a calendar. Week forty-five. New moon. Phone Wednesday night. What about old phone? Who follows who on the page? The last of love the leaves a winding sheet in the trees. We kiss — but our lips are old photos of dogs. Silence is destroyed by blackbirds. They are not birds. There are no birds. Take one pill three times a day. They don't just treat the symptoms they treat the causes. We are moving toward a complete reclassification. It has the power to make us all better workers. The stones and pebbles bury each other by the sea. By the road. By the nuclear power station. Police siren through open window. Police siren through closed window. Sparrows feeding through open window. Sparrows feeding through closed window. Children playing through open window. Children playing through closed window. Car starting through open window. Car starting through closed window. A rook sits in the recently ploughed field as a tractor with a hay baler attached drives around the field in gradually decreasing circles until it drives in the smallest circle that it is possible for it to travel in. The bales of hay lie in the dust and heat of late summer. The smell of instant coffee on teacher's breath. The light was extremely brilliant and painful. Then describe again and again and so on and so on for several pages each description laid over the other. *The best part will go into the fire.* A dream: The footpath was clear but I could not move along it. I took out my notebook and drew a line and walked my fingers along it and then I went home but my home was not there so I drew a picture of my home and lay across it. When I woke up I was so embarrassed that I rubbed out the line and the drawing of my home. I gathered up all of the eraser rubbings and I put them in a glass vial so that I would never forget my embarrassment. But now the wheat field is covered in tarpaulin. The rooks and jackdaws gather on the stacks. They are watching us rain from the sky. Things that used to be human. I am conscious of the fact that I have written the end at the beginning or at least near the beginning and the only way to rectify it is to try and forget about such notions as beginning middle and end. To that end I write from inside the work itself. The wind speaks through the trees. There is no need to elaborate. After the rain: A buzzard calling. After the rain: A cat calling. After the rain: An unknown number. After the rain: Specific units of structure. After the rain: An old metal bridge. In the pocket of my jeans I find a note that reads: *Beautiful damned sea of not water*. I have no memory of writing it but I recognise my handwriting. This discovery leaves me empty. Though because I am empty I do not recognise it at first. Empty according to the 1990 edition of the Collins Paperback English Dictionary is your body suggesting the space that surrounds it. Because I am from Lincolnshire I have learnt to recognise emptiness. Sighing in Lincolnshire is very different to sighing in London or Leeds but it is also exactly the same. In Lincolnshire the sky melts into your body so that you can never escape. I have been wanting to tell this story for years but now I realise that I don't want to tell this story so I just let it shine through the cracks. The spaces. The white words. The white white words. Stones and pebbles bury each other by the sea. Embankment to embankment. Red and yellow roses on a black background. Swallows gather above the Rhee Wall above the sound mirrors above the train yard. Street light through open window. Street light through closed window. Cherry tree through open window. Cherry tree through closed window.

Friends talking through open window. Friends talking through closed window. Leaves through open window. Leaves through closed window. In a democracy everyone is trained to suspect everybody else. If you don't suspect everybody else you are not allowed to live in a democracy. The wind speaks through the trees. There is no need to elaborate. The truth is I am broken. I am searching for spiderwebs carried on warm air. None of these words are mine. They are ours. What does this say if anything about my state of mind. The truth is those last few lines have been written over. They are not the first and they will not be the last. They are ours. In liberty and revolution. As in turning. As in a wheel. As in against straight lines and perpendiculars. I wake up suddenly in the middle of summer and our hands are made of feathers and dust. Remember: No one is allowed to live in a democracy. Our bodies. The factory. Sunlight. In classical Chinese poetry wild geese are a symbol of distant love. Of separation. Of yearning to return. In this poem however they are simply wild geese flying over the dunes as I drive to work. Beautiful and alive in the world and part of us. Of all of us. Embankment to embankment. A silence. At work I am stripping paint from the windows of an eighteenth-century farmhouse. There are many layers. White and green and green and black and finally down to the bare wood. To fill to sand to paint again. The windows. I eat English cherries in the rain and there are no boundaries. No borders. Only human beings and good fortunes. I sweep up the fragments of paint and dust and splinters. I sweep them up using a hard-bristled broom and then I sweep them into a dustpan and empty them into a bin bag. I place the bin bag into a skip in the front garden and later on the skip company pick it up and haul it to landfill. It is buried along with everything else that we know and care for. Damaged negatives held up to the sun. Within the landfill so many things of apparent beauty. At the weekend I chop logs in thirty-degree heat. It is September and summer has come late. I do not want an identity. What do you want? I want symbols. Crow is symbol. Water is symbol. Brick wall is symbol. Sky is symbol. Mouth is symbol. It is not symbol. Nothing is symbol. Nothing is simple. It is so so simple. You said: The best place to see the stars is from your own back garden. It is so so simple. Stones and pebbles bury each other by the nuclear power station. After the rain: A Dog barking. After the rain: A power cut. After the rain: The lighthouse. After the rain: Jackdaws. After the rain: An old metal bin. In my coat pocket I find a note that reads: *It is not a symbol it is a sign.* I can remember writing it but I do not recognise my handwriting. This discovery scares me. I am with fear. Again and again I am with fear. Fear according to the 1990 edition of the Collins Paperback English Dictionary is a visitation of birds singing in a dead oak. They are long-tailed tits. It is not a symbol it is a sign. And our mothers dying so far apart. It is not a symbol it is a sign. A river. An ocean. A cup of blue glass. We sit in the summer house watching the butterflies the bees the blue blue sky and the deer tracks. The wind speaks through the trees. Cats fighting through open window. Cats fighting through closed window. Rain falling through open window. Rain falling through closed window. Cyclists through open window. Cyclists through closed window. Lawnmower through open window. Lawnmower through closed window. Modulated sounds drifting toward us the waves changed by the topography of the valley. Peaks and troughs roughshod along lanes and along fields and within abandoned garages. *The best part will go into the fire.* I am raining in Ivychurch I am raining in Newchurch I am raining in Rye and Camber and Dungeness. All of the forces falling (striating the sand) and falling again. Pieces of this and that our empty faces made over in circles of forgetting. The scriptural references contain sharp holy light in a letter now lost. All of the letters are lost. The dark dark the clear dark which does not allow even the faintest trace of humanity to endure. Circle of ice. Circle of flame. Circle of earth. There is a half-finished magpie scribbled out on the sea wall. It is a circle of beginning and ending. Nothing but a car engine turning over in the dark. I am conscious of the fact that I have written the beginning at the end or at least near the end and the only way to rectify it is to try and forget about such notions as beginning middle and end. To that end I write from inside the work itself. On Wednesdays I used to go to the outlet centre before the shops opened and walk around listening to the birds. One day somebody followed me home so I drove to a village that I had never been to before and hid in the cemetery until the person following me drove away. I must tell you that I do not like the sound of blood when I can hear it on television. I only like bruises and that is why I like Japanese films more than European films. The blood sounds different and the bruises are better. It is very effective in treating PTSD. They don't just treat the symptoms they treat the causes. We are moving toward a complete reclassification. It has the power to make us all better workers. Looking out over the marsh: An asymmetrical arrangement of street lights. Looking out over the marsh: Bare winter trees. Looking out over the marsh: Seagulls following a tractor as it ploughs the back field. One black thread and one red thread. Crystallised dew covers the grass and the hawthorn and the spiderwebs. Elms grow in the hedgerows but rarely grow into tall trees around these parts due to disease. Early morning sunlight on gorse. The only true yellow. A burning yellow of half-sleep. *The best part will go into the fire.* At least fifteen magpies in the hawthorn. The field in which it sits is completely covered in brambles and bindweed. Swallows in late September fly around the old grain silo on Wenhams Lane. Looking out across the fields: Deer tracks and greenbottles and pheasant. For a moment a thousand vertical rainbows. For a moment burning harvest stubble. For a moment the sound of shingle. For a moment frozen sea against skin. For a moment wild rosemary edge of sheep field. A bee so heavily laden with pollen it can barely fly. Power moving down the lines. Last breath with spider. Last breath with sheep. Last breath with crops and wild flowers and garden. Looking out over the fields the valley the woods. *The best part will go into the fire.* The garden the rays of light the mice the spiders the wind. For a moment a cow lowing in the darkness. For a moment no beginning and no end. For a moment sheep pulling fresh grass. We hold on to the image too long. Too long against the sea. The red flag of mourning. This is not the end of something it is more like the beginning. I know it is not the end because at the end I wrote about how I prefer poems to stories because in poems you always know where you are. You are right here reading a poem and it is about nothing and everything at the same time. We are nothing and everything at the same time. Put match to paper and dry grass until a thick dark smoke moves over the valley. Just this moment. And then nothing at all. *The best part will go into the fire.*

SECTOR LIGHTS

We look out over the ocean as the light shifts into morning grey. We are taken by it. With it. Neither of us are one of us. Instead nothing. A tangle of tall trees. There is no one. Only a comfortable surrender to the inevitable. Walking beach. Pebbles underfoot. The self disintegrates. Melting into the constantly shifting stones. In the fetters. In the rope. In the rose. Regrets turn into absence. The rifle shells. I lose all sense of days. Oak leaf. Old stone wall. Rain adding to a puddle. Old stone wall. Earthworm moving across pavement. Old stone wall. We are praying for a world without words. All species working together. Mutually assured destruction. Light makes its own language upon water. Upon windows. Upon wet stones. We are swimming in white light. We are swimming in red light. We are swimming in green light. From each wave we move on to the next — swallowing water and air and sand and stones and dust. I pick up a torch and I put it in my pocket. I forget about it for a while and then I go out on my own and drive three miles in the dark so that I can shine the white torchlight on the back of my hand in private. I shine the white torchlight on the back of my hand. I feel better. I talk of this to no one. Pylons hum with electricity in the rain. The lanes are full of umbellifers — mostly cow parsley — but there are areas that are studded with hemlock — most readily discernable by their blotchy green and purple stems. On the back roads between Old Romney and Lydd is a ruin — only one wall with arched window standing. I run for hours and hear no one. Hear nothing. As I recall: Pebbles and lighthouse and stone. As I recall: Sea kale and black-headed gulls and white horses. As I recall: Bricks and chrysalis and ragwort. As I recall: Sleepers and carriages and slabs of concrete. As I recall: Fishing nets and power station and rifle shells. A heron flies overhead frame by frame. We are mud and sandcastles. We fill up with brine and seaweed. Cherry blossoms cover the windscreen. I lose all sense of adverse days. The words turn back into dead leaves and stones. We are son and daughter and mother — never father — further from. The wet feathers are blown away by wind. The wind blows it all away. There are longer passages between rocks and sandbars which remain the same. The same always so that we may notice change. Themes fade beyond the reach of senses. I reach beyond the cup the glass the cold torque of water resisting touch. I count the old money the old pennies the quarters the lira. The pennies are non-decimal. I cannot comprehend the maths. I celebrate the foreign. The plastic. The unknown. I lose all sense of adverse days. Cherry tree. Elder. The shadow of a cactus. I suppose I am exhausted as I can no longer read the letters of the artists. Oak leaf. Old stone wall. Oak leaf. Old stone wall. We can see the power station in the near distance and pylons again stretching into the sea. Sometimes I feel that we are digging only to escape the hole. We are spade and dirt and we have no fingers. We are swimming in white light. We are swimming in red light. We are swimming in green light. Along the canal — reeds are still against water. Clouds move ever so slowly. A car drives past frame by frame. Two sets of transmission lines stand in water marching slowly across the Denge. There is a weak shingle bank nearby that often leads to flooding. What is friendship? It is a seabird feeding by the lighthouse. We record seeds and names and lines. We record wind and flower and fable. We record apple and peach and orange. You make a mark in the wet concrete and then take a photograph of the shadows cast by the power lines upon the green and yellow fields. They are almost indistinguishable from animal tracks but they appear to be more like words written down on a page which also look like footprints going nowhere. Nothing. Emptiness. This is the light we are looking for. The sea deposits objects of a similar size and weight in the same troughs. A line of bottles a line of ropes a line of driftwood. All that is body is ebb and flow. All that is body is sky and river. All that is body is flooding plain. Then humiliated I murmured: *The sea the sea*. Outlined by sun against white background. At home I noticed a mark on the wall that looked as if it could have been made by the claw of a hammer while someone was removing a picture hook. I ran my finger over the mark several times trying to get a feel for it. It was an indentation. Not quite a hole. I filled it and sanded it and primed it and painted it and now it is no longer visible. It is my intention to swim this evening.

It is my intention to drink whisky on the shore. Do they know about the other lovers? The sea fucking the sand and the birds and the stones and the fish and the flesh and all of us atoms trailing in the aftermath. Light et cetera. Painting et cetera. Water et cetera. The old lighthouse and the new lighthouse. We don't know anything about the past because people in the past didn't write anything down. Only the stones that we cannot understand. Advance and retire. The ancient dance of the sea. Advance and retire followed by the made-up names of birds. For birds. Everything is for the birds. Advance and retire the torn yellow days. The skies smudged by the wet thumb of a child. To suck the thumb — the sea — the birds — the pebbles — the dust — the torn yellow days. To suck paper and ink and sand and stone. I cut my nails my hair my eyebrows and suck them in the driveway in the rain. I think of you and it puts me together. Now adders. A temporal space. I place everything inside my body face down on the table and then a worm eaten. Move over my love is over and then we learn to pick up sticks. We learn to read the branches of the willow. We walk down an unmetalled road the shadows of clouds moving over the moor. I am indeed a blackbird. To suck paper and ink and stones. We have no distinguishing features. Light cuts boiled light. Light cuts sacred light. Light cuts light light. And in the doorway you are stoned. Several stones on top of one another. An avalanche in waiting. An old stone wall. Oak leaf. Rain adding to a puddle. Old stone wall. I am indeed a rook — a jackdaw — a miscellany of deeds. They have erected a temporary barrier — they think of me and put you together. Who else can we imagine the look on the face of? A line of flowering hawthorn dividing two fields of wheat. Advance and retire the made-up names of birds. I am friends with buzzard and blackthorn and ash. With hornbeam and deer and lichen. I am friends with voice and mud and pond. With acorn and glass and sunlight. With language and dog and root systems. With bodies and sweat and loose clothing. I am friends with comets. I am friends with the afterlife. I am friends with clouds and razors and painkillers. I am friends with books. With water. With black smoke and burning stubble. I am reading *The Story of Lighthouses and Lightships and Lifeboats*. Show a white tower against dark cliffs. Show a black banded tower against white cliffs. Show a red tower against the sky. Show a red and white tower against sky and sea. Trinity lighthouse at Dungeness contains sixty loudspeaker units which provide an electric fog signal. The fog signal is automatically operated by the fog detector. We are nothing on earth. Nothing fits into nothing. We are nothing on earth. Rain falling on corrugated plastic. Rain falling on bamboo. Rain falling on frozen water. Rain falling on sand. Rain falling on paper. There are times that I become bird. Become buzzard. Become red kite. Become kestrel. The wet feathers are blown away by wind. The wind blows it all away. The window widow spins its web and you feed it flies as a storm approaches. Pink lightning from cumulonimbus. We are shattered. Remaining nevertheless. Light cuts moonlight. Light cuts school light. Light cuts bus light. Words spare on one syllable. The occasion of monoplace written as a postscript to great dangers. Found faded forgotten orders. You sip from a chipped cup. It is a green mug not a cup. It has a hairline fracture running from where the handle meets the body to the base. There is no chip. A hairline fracture runs through light and words and touch. Sometimes a sentence becomes a word. Sometimes a sentence becomes a world. A sentence is such. Is just. We are swimming in white light. We are swimming in red light. We are swimming in green light. Later on I walk for a few miles along the footpaths over the Denge toward the shingle. I find an empty goldfinch nest dislodged by wind. I pick it up and carry it home with great care. It is so soft. It is made of twigs and grasses and lichen and moss. I keep it in my pocket for several weeks until it becomes unmade and I play with the twigs and the grasses and the lichen and the moss. I move them between my fingers and think of the wind. I am blown apart by it. Light cuts star light. Light cuts porch light. Light cuts fairground light. You once said that the present is a future that the past made up. I erase the future. It is a language that I no longer speak. My distance is so long above ground. A temporary barrier.

Driving along the Military Road in the rain — sky and land are one continuous space. The road runs alongside the Royal Military Canal for several miles. There are times that I become bird. Become buzzard. Become red kite. Become kestrel. Wing touching water. Wing touching cloud. Wing touching wheat. I have to resist the transformation whilst driving. Especially in the rain. Light through yellow glass. Light through red glass. Light through white glass. I have no doubt about the borderland between Kent and East Sussex. I have no doubt because I understand the complexity of the vacuum. It is a liminal space in which time mingles with sunlight upon water. Glass. Mirror. Body of ice. Light returned by a reflective surface. Sound also returns as will be shown later. Acrylic. Charcoal. Dust. I suppose that is our allotment. Sky and sea and solitary gull. It is all we have. It is all we know. The motion of lovers — the windows will win in reflection. For instance — all objects are also shadows. A few days later I walk along the beach at Littlestone collecting plastic bottle tops and small pieces of driftwood. A mixture of sand and stone underfoot. The tide is in. I stop every hundred metres or so and draw an ampersand on the shoreline with a stick. Seagulls are fighting over the carcass of a dogfish. An eye eaten away. The sea is still and clear. Reflection of stone. Reflection of sky. Reflection of rain. Everything comes back to water. The voices underfoot. The words upon the page. If you were reborn it would be as a yellow horned poppy against shingle. We want the other to be at the edge. The centre is reserved for loss. The sun shines through a stained-glass window. We trace the wandering stars. Release sky and gravel and rain. Release sunlight and ash and elm. Here lies the body of virtue. Here lies the body of youth. The day begins in centrifuge. No narrative just high-pitched tones and isolated images ascending and descending as if in a pattern. This is our poetry winding down. The edge of days. The aegis of rooks. A quiet supplication in this liminal space. We are swallowing white light. We are swallowing red light. We are swallowing green light.

I was going to write about the sound mirrors at Greatstone but things fell apart.

I was going to write about St Thomas Becket Church at Fairfield but things fell apart.

I was going to write about the sunken forest at Pett Level but things fell apart.

I was going to write about the view from the top of the old lighthouse at Dungeness but things fell apart.

I was going to write more about the sea but things fell apart.

(The sea is pushing against us)

I envy the lighthouse.
I envy the light.

(The sea is pushing against us)

Against the past.

Against each other.

What's passed

cannot be written down.

IN THE HOUSE OF
KEEPING STILL

Yesterday I spoke of today / speak of nothing at all. In your company return. Return to your company. In faces. Our faces faces. Will you go by? Move aside? The private life of ash. They say it is a place. A blessing. In the old days we held ourselves under the sea. I have a distant idea. A forthcoming. That on one side of a black hole we write and on the other we are written down. Low wet ground. Traces of iron slag and pesticides. Abandoned farm buildings in silhouette or a compact layer of broken flint. I am wrapped in a blanket drinking red wine and eating Moroccan hash. I write a poem called *Dropping ecstasy at the end of the world* and then I destroy it. I burn it on the fire. I walk across the marsh toward the peninsula — toward the blue sky. Neither of us slept during the late frost. Under tree a skin forming. Acres of solar panels in the old sheep field. A minuet. A kestrel. The early morning light. A drone through cleavers. A drone through willow. A drone through birch and hornbeam. When will I see you? Perhaps we have missed the exact set of coordinate points at which we were destined to meet? They say it is a place. A blessing. One foot in front of another foot in a turn-of-the-century photograph. I think about the time when somebody stopped us in the street and asked if we were practising a dance and we didn't know how to answer so we didn't say anything at all. That must be everyone fallen out with everyone. The way the light falls on a plastic plate in the back room. It attracts insects and nobody says a word. You can tell when something bad is about to happen by the type of music they play beforehand. It is often a sustained chord in a minor key but occasionally it is more rhythmical. Everything seemed so final in the past but it has not yet happened. It is by no means for certain. When we dropped the glass between us it held in the air for several seconds and then shattered in slow motion. When glass breaks it is a sign that you need to make immediate changes to your environment.

A garden spider moved into the house and built a web near the window from which the first bluebottle of summer escaped before it could be eaten. This must be the best possible world of all possible worlds.

Early morning. Lower field. Evidence of ceremony. Nothing can travel faster than the speed of light but the dark doesn't have to travel at all because it is already here. Words tower above us though they are not words they are buildings. Today we are projected through blue glass onto the wings of city pigeons. You are supposed to ask a question first but many people have no idea what it is that they want to know until they are told by someone else.

On one side of a black hole we live and on the other we are painted on fabric. Sometimes our hands touch and sometimes they don't. I cut my tongue in the rain — but nothing mattered — I was dream-bitten.

I walked from Hamstreet to Ashford to meet you by the Outlet Centre where we processed our emotions using two sides of the material divide. Our body patterns are roads buried under centuries of dust. Language enzymes parking in target bodies. A collective assumption. There's a lot that I do to come back / inside other people. Dialogue / a process of abstraction. Fucked on crystals so a morning. Multiply in the silt. At any moment return my words over yours. Reaching stars. A habit repeated in nature. We circle a wind-up crow. How fingers write. The speed of dab. Water as condensation. Time moving between us. So many voices. To feel your heartbeat underwater unnerves spider flank. Through driftwood a deck hand. Card against card unversed. The web aces dark. If chance is kindness then branch a running tide. Our bodies talk aft. This estuary figure. Being that we collect bones we cannot look back. This is not my voice by the way. I promise you it is not my voice. It is someone else's voice and I cannot get rid of it. They choose to speak through me because I am completely empty and I have no words. When I look around I see the world through a grid and that way I am able to ensure that everything is in proportion to everything else and that whatever I am looking at is seen from the correct perspective.

When I took the last letter you sent me out of the envelope I noticed a scrap of paper stuck in the corner. On one side it read: *Language helps itself and itself only.* And on the other: *They no longer speak to us we are cast out among the forest dwellers.* Molten wax poured into water in an effort to foretell the future.

It is of no use now. We talk in the caravan for hours. You said there were no words left. Nothing but birdsong over evening mist. We stand opposite each other writing the day into a dull chapel and one of us notices a plume of black smoke being carried over the sea.

When we took down the walls we found boxes of paper with writing on every sheet. It was common practice not so long ago to write a particular word or group of words on paper and then eat the words over a period of time to prevent illness or reduce fever. The next day we piled up all of the paper in the field at the bottom of the valley and set it alight. We looked at each other in disgust understanding intuitively the negative forces lurking within all structures.

When I was a child I thought the phrase *round of applause* was *ramble of floors* and when I watched game shows with my family and the audience applauded I imagined that they were stamping their feet upon a wooden stage. I also believed that the sound of canned laughter was created by a group of people sitting with trays of shattered glass on their laps moving a rolling pin back and forth over the shards to create the desired effect. This must be the best possible world of all possible worlds.

Sooner or later the dream fades and we are left alone to learn sign language. On the banks of a river we punish each other with maximum pressure and total shame. For this I blame the other world. I cannot sleep. I lie in bed thinking about the day the bed was delivered and about how long it took us to put it together. There were a couple of bolts missing — but this does not seem to have caused any significant problems. The red sun breaks through in morning. I know it is morning by the way the birds are singing because they sing differently in the morning than they do at night. If you played me a recording of birds singing at night and then a recording of birds singing in the morning I would be able to tell you which recording was of birds singing at night and which recording was of birds singing in the morning. Whatever this is it is not the same as writing it is more like the cutting of the fields.

A line drawn around the sky. A line drawn around the stars. A line drawn around the shadows.

You started getting migraines after the fire but somehow the migraines gave you the ability to communicate with jackdaws. Early morning. Lower field. Evidence of fox kill. A drone through rain. A drone through bracken. A drone through hemlock and reedmace. You are supposed to ask a question first but many people have no idea what it is that they want to know until they are told by someone else. The timeline splits when we make a decision — or when someone else makes a decision that affects our decision-making process. What we think of as a line travelling from *a* to *b* is actually a circle going nowhere.

A garden spider moved into the house and built a web near the window from which the first bluebottle of summer could not escape before it was eaten. This must be the best possible world of all possible worlds.

The bend of starlight. The stillness of the past. It is raining vinegar. It is raining tiny versions of ourselves. It is raining feathers and plastic and ink. We brought back panic and cleaver kings on the eve of the eve of a blood moon. This is it: A moving error. A blade of grass. A dock leaf. I tore up all the letters you ever sent me and then I tried to piece them all together again. It is raining fortune-telling miracle fish. It is raining mirrors.

It is raining all of the things we have said and done.

I cannot remember what I am. What am I doing. O yes.

The terror. *I bite my poem until it bleeds.* They say it is a place. A blessing. Feet on grass explode cliffs. Towers open dry-ice chambers at dusk. The landing smells of sleep and vagabond canals and we look out over town at the old malt kiln — at the cloud cuckoos and the counter-clocks. Obelisks in the sky / give me a break / it's just a storm approaching. It runs in your mother's family in (electric) yellow light. Dust and gas and rock. The gravity of it all. The waiting.

A FELL DESTROYER

The sun falls through the window in a sliver of light. It is trying to get inside me. That is what the sun does. It tries to get inside me and if it does get inside me I will become a two-dimensional shape in the clear sky of knowing and I do not want to become a two-dimensional shape in the clear sky of knowing. The sun is ninety-three million miles away from the earth and its light takes roughly eight minutes and twenty seconds to reach us so when we look at the sun we are always looking at the past. I try to write every day but more often than not the sunlight hits the page and the words do not come — or they come and then they disappear. The speed of light in a vacuum is a universal physical constant. It moves at approximately one hundred and eighty-six thousand miles per second. The last time I saw you you asked me if I was going to talk to my friends about it and I told you that none of my friends gave a shit — but the truth of the matter is that I do not want to talk to anyone about anything. We sat on the beach watching the reflection of light the refraction of light the diffraction of light the interference of light the polarisation of light the dispersion of light and the scattering of light. Talking about light is like trying to plot the coordinates of a dream in the middle of the night. Surely our sun from which no secrets are hidden should select a judge or should allow us to judge ourselves? A wave of light knocks me through the wall into a room that I never knew existed. A great terror in the weight of an unknown language. If this is reality it is also an oblivion of sorts. These atoms fail me both inside and out. What an outpouring they will say.

O dirt of my body.

O grinding of teeth.

I would like to collapse in the park but it is not possible to collapse in the park and the clouds keep coming and the clouds keep coming — it is deadpan normal — it is same-feel with glass doors uneven spiders. Conversations with you never seem to begin exactly because you so often slip into a silent contemplation from which you cannot be roused. The thought of you pushing open the double doors into wet sunlight (nowhere but nowhere) — I was a vapour trail of worry.

Lost in

the bright morning.

In order to continue our dialogue somehow in the room that I discovered we enter into a covenant though it is not officially recognised by a governing body. Moments like this are devoid of beauty and integrity. I stand outside of time — a flower in reverse. Beyond all atoms and molecules there are one-dimensional strings that vibrate. These vibrations include the three-dimensional space we live in plus time and language. Try opening the epiphany windows to see if that makes you feel any better. People come from miles around to open the windows and it often changes their lives. If you ever come to live in the clear sky of knowing I suggest that you put a cloud in it and remember nothing. For this one I lay it bare because I have nothing left to hide and no reason to hide it. A beam of light falls through the curtains onto a stack of unread books passing over a couple of drawings as it does so. One of the drawings is in charcoal and consists of a single abstract shape that was created by writing the word *sun* over and over itself one hundred times. The other drawing is in pencil and black chalk and graphite marker and is made up of a four-columned grid that contains various examples of unreadable handwritten statements. A while ago I moved into a caravan in a sheep field and I have become obsessed with the view over the valley through the small square window. I spend a lot of time watching the dusk approach and then turn into darkness and in the morning I watch the mist rise and the fog descend. One evening I used my phone to take a photograph of the view over the valley through the small square window and a few days later I had the photograph printed as an 8 x 8 image and I stuck it to the wall next to the small square window using Blu Tack and now when I look through the small square window over the valley I can also see the photograph of the view through the small square window over the valley. A few days later I took another photograph of the view over the valley through the small square window that included the photograph of the view over the valley through the small square window. I had the photograph printed as an 8 x 8 image which I stuck to the wall   next to the small square window using Blu Tack and now when I look through the small square window over the valley I can also see the photograph of the view through the small square window over the valley and the photograph of the photograph of the view through the small square window over the valley. I continued to do this for several weeks until there were twenty-four photographs of the view through the small square window over the valley which also contained within them the photographs and the photographs of the photographs of the view through the small square window over the valley. Two figures swap places with the rain. As far as the eye cannot see. It is a matter of finding our position within a certain point of view. That we do not know and we do not know.

To take up speech

and let it go.

Without past present or future tense my pronouns stink of capitalism. Of an utter lack of articulation. As if the word itself was the dead of a thing. Anything. Anything at all. Any old iron thing that stalks the hallways of the worst that there is to remember. I am a died in the wall bloody goody two shoes and I predict that we will all corrode in real time. Since memory is an event train I need you to explain the granularity of the concept. We talk in the ante meridiem whispering dark notifications to one another along the crackle of the line. Since memory. Since nothing. Since our exile and communion with landfill. Fuck-knuckles lagging in the afterglow.

Then sunlight

& dust.

At work I pick up sections of rotten wood and old putty and oil paint that I have removed from the windows and I put it all into a bag and when I get home I empty the contents of the bag into a box frame and hang it on the wall and I stare at it for several hours. After a while I realise that I am looking into the thing that I used to look through and I am dumbfounded.

Burning and

      burning and

doubling and doubling.

              I don't know where to start so I begin everywhere and then I realise that you are talking to me from the grave and my mouth is full of ash my own ash from the burning of my body. I think about all the things that could happen but I do not want to think about anything anymore. Even the things that happened in the past. Especially the things that happened in the past — and then I catch myself in the glass — a mad bastard in the last rays.

A few days ago you asked me what I wanted to do next

and I said get a new body and you said when you get a new body you can look out over the valley again. I do not want to look out over the valley again. I want something to mitigate it. Something systemic not topical. I draw spiral patterns with multiple pencils and then a ruled line and then one hundred non-ruled lines. It makes no difference to anything at all. It is nothing. Distant this. Distant that. Even my dog face between windows. When a lorry drives past it could suck you under if it is driving too fast and if you are walking too close to the road. It is full of light and water and glass. I am now going to show you how to tie a knot in a length of rope without letting go of either end. You have to fold your arms before you pick up the rope and the act of unfolding them will appear to produce a knot. But to accomplish this you have to let go of one end of the rope for the briefest of moments. As the hands are brought together to drop off the loops that encircle them one hand releases one end and regains it at the same point after it has passed through one of the loops. The releasing and regaining of the end blurs together in a continuous movement to give the impression that each end of the rope has been held throughout the process. It is full of light and water and plastic. Why not defend me in your mother's voice? Your mother's voice in a small room and your mother's voice in a big room. In a dream. In circular columns of darkness. Fields bordered by sunflowers. I do not like to talk about it. Through the camera zoom we can see tiny orbs being ejected from the main luminosity. Sky burns away. Metal in the early days. Not this language — only echoes of the changes in light. The river things / my bread-and-butter saint. O the fuckery of it all. A misery chord in the chest. I am sleeping real good at night because I do not have any limitations. If you have limitations you will not sleep good at night. I map the light and the shadows but I do not know the ways in which the light and shadows act. It is nothing personal — I just don't like the way the word feels in my mouth. A voice: *Nothing being. Nothing done. On rocks — on birds — an ocean.* I listen to the voice over and over sat in a café at a table with a crooked leg. Backwards and forwards — the rocking back and forth. It was all an act. The back and forth. A constant to and fro. The source unknown. Random spots of colour. I am working on becoming a truly immoral being — but to do this I must escape all human limits. Calm down. A piano. A cello. A violin. I catch tatterdemalion trees. In toil the leaves spent might. The red sun breaks through in morning. We cannot move. The red sun breaks through in morning. Do not say anything. Do not say anything at all. If you do our lives will fall apart they will fall apart completely. Utterly and completely they will fall apart. The next thing I know I am saying the thing that I am not meant to say. I have made it at last. Beyond human limits. Your own impression would be quite different because even in three dimensions we automatically treat it as a two-dimensional shape. I am sorry that I can only offer these little sketches at present. I know they do not look like much but they are in fact a direct route to the other side. *Arbitrary figures under dissolved bridges. You must forget weakness / the stranglehold.* Now we are downriver. A box of temazepam palmed between us. A sideways glance. A touch of hand. When trees are dehydrated they sometimes make popping and cracking sounds as they attempt to draw water up through their roots. To a certain extent we are all victims of expectation. You once asked me to translate the sound of wind moving through trees which I did by recording the sound of wind moving through trees and digitally manipulating it until it sounded like the string section of an orchestra and you said that is not a translation you have destroyed the music of the trees and I replied that all translations are acts of destruction. At any moment anything can turn around by chance. A bridge being closed or the words returning once again to glass. A poem is not a hymn. A poem is not magic. It is the most ordinary thing laid bare. Then an image of an industrial landscape placed over a completely sterile environment. Venom laws. A bridge being opened. I scrape off the old oil paint and the putty and dig out the rotten wood and then I fill the surface and sand it to make it flat. There is so much work to do. A crow with resting bitch face on the scaffold. Let's take the house down and use the bricks to build a wall. A wall around us. A wall around us all. There is no community just a bunch of people who will like you if you are like them and hate you if you are not. It is the shadow work in the rust belt that will bring us together not the distant karaoke of dogs. We make up all this stuff about nature. Bedfellows in a world without rain. To be left outside a bird. In for. In forgetting. I forget. A name withheld. A letter withdrawn. An essay all but destroyed. The moving image is silent. A darkness seeping through. We stand still within the frames of a biological film. There are things that fundamentally elude us. Elide into one moment. Inside the world it feels different — like how the house functions when you are no longer in it.

How are you feeling today?

All to hell. All to hell. There is something ridiculous about misery. Goodbye my loveds. Seven sparrows — August 22nd — 2005. A little twitch of willow. A fuck by the sea.

At the Museum of Purgatory in Rome there is a photocopy of a burn mark left by a Madame Leleux on the sleeve of her son Joseph's shirt. According to the son he heard noises for eleven consecutive nights that terrified him so much that he vomited. On the twelfth night his mother appeared to him and laid her hand on his shirt — leaving a visible print.

It is a colour field of language — a blackout normal. Revolve around them in linguistic confusion — forever turning. Amen.

I woke up in the nineteenth century and discovered that I had no voice and then I heard a chorus of children in the distance: *We play hide and seek but nobody hides. We are all searching — nothing to find. Win all the marbles / mist on water. To be left outside a bird. I take my life and lay it under an oak tree. Say quiet things aloud. Sing with me collapsing stars. Storm cells. Curses. Sunlight.* When

I look at a map I find it hard to tell which part is land and which part is sea — just like I find it hard to tell the difference between my body and the sky. Glint of metal in the distance. Rooks pecking at fallen apples. Ghost hawthorn by the wire fence. It is a closed country for me though I am not yet seeking human language. In fact I am better at going backwards than going forwards because when I am going forwards I cannot see where I have been. Do you realise that many things will fall away unless we talk about films or mention all the books we've read? I'm sorry — I did not hear you because the sun hit me and the light scabbed over but even if I did hear you I probably would have pretended that I had not. It is okay — just concentrate on the road. When I first drove here I did not know where I was going and I did not know when to turn off — but now that I have been here several times I know where I am going and I know when to turn off.

Star

burning

above.

Yes I was twatted as I walked through the ruins after an all-night rave in an abandoned quarry in Rochdale. I had run off on my own because the pink morning light was calling me closer and closer and I was trying to become part of it somehow. To them it should not have mattered but it did matter — it mattered more than anything had ever mattered before. Before hand. Before body. Before language.

I woke up suddenly in the middle of summer a series of absences stacked up next to each other against a white wall.

Who are you?

I am simply a field of aesthetic possibilities whose

purpose it is to lie here and dream.

What do you look like?

I see myself in others.

What do I look like?

Pigeons circling and returning.

What is your earliest memory?

I experience everything at once so I have no need for memory.

A cup of coffee

in the waking light.

In China recent experiments in nuclear fusion resulted in an artificial sun running at seventy million degrees Celsius for twenty minutes. The temperature of the earth's sun ranges from ten to fifteen million degrees Celsius and it has been active for over four and a half billion years. It formed from the gravitational collapse of matter within an interstellar cloud. But in the department of restricted books I found only maps of the stars created out of the stars themselves. What if this world exists within another world — and that other world within another — and so on and so on and so on? About us

(words bring)

draw to

a close.

I walk into the sea with a belly full of Valium as the porcelain misters call my name. It is a raid on the uncanny. An act of malfeasance. We are laughing and smiling at people off camera as they stand in the long bodies of water left by the receding tide. Eventually the shadow world of last night's bottle returns and there is a slight change of plan. You may someday realise that my anger is an unspoken thing. But what I am really trying to say and what I have always been trying to say is let the light be light.

Your name is paper to me

gently put down

and your story

is wing dust over trees

How the other half cuts skin makes sense in the thread-
world. Beginning beginning to talk like me. Just as
fingertips touch water — I spit up into the sky and it
sticks.

A new moon in suburbia.

ACKNOWLEDGEMENTS

Extracts from earlier versions of this text have appeared in the following publications:

Futch Press, Long Poem Magazine, Eratio, Fieldnotes.

A book is never written alone. The following people have helped whether they realise it or not:

Leah Epton, Rainer Clarke Emmerson, Noel Guinan, Chris Stephenson, Tom Jenks, James Davies, Keira Greene, Ellen James, Lucy Harvest Clarke, Sam Whitcombe, Mark Rice, Kim Ekin, Gilly Clarke, Christine Bellamy, George and Anita, Nigel Greene, Chris Thompson, Scott Thurston, Andy Moore, Jenny Tucker, The Eggs, and Simon Savage – 1977 – 2021 – you mad beautiful bastard.

Special thanks to Richard Makin for reading previous versions of this text, invaluable assistance with spelling and grammar, and many a night down the tavern.

LAY OUT YOUR UNREST

Milton Keynes UK
Ingram Content Group UK Ltd.
UKHW022236130624
444101UK00005BA/94

9 781916 938175